VOLUME 1

HOW GOD USED ME IN AN EXTRAORDINARY AND MIRACULOUS WAYS TO BLESS OTHERS

"To God Be the Glory"

MARIE E. WILLIAMSON

Order this book online at www.trafford.com
or email orders@trafford.com

Most Trafford titles are also available at major online book retailers.

Scripture quotations marked KJV are from the Holy Bible, King James Version
(Authorized Version). First published in 1611. Quoted from the KJV Classic
Reference Bible, Copyright © 1983 by The Zondervan Corporation.

Print information available on the last page.

ISBN: 978-1-4907-5207-5 (sc)
ISBN: 978-1-4907-5209-9 (hc)
ISBN: 978-1-4907-5208-2 (e)

Library of Congress Control Number: 2014921522

Trafford rev. 04/08/2015

Trafford PUBLISHING® www.trafford.com
North America & international
toll-free: 1 888 232 4444 (USA & Canada)
fax: 812 355 4082

To God be the glory.

This book is dedicated to my Lord and Savior, Jesus Christ, whom I love dearly with all my heart, soul, might, and strength. I was able to publish this book by the inspiration and guidance of my Lord, Jesus, who is my encourager, counselor, and loyal Father. He has taught me to watch and pray.

To God be the glory!

Expression of my gratitude toward the Lord Jesus Christ.

Jesus, When Will I See You
Jesus, I need all of You,
then I can see You,
then I can get to heaven.
Oh, Jesus, I need all of You.

My King on the Throne
Jesus is my King on the throne.
Jesus, You are my King in authority.
Jesus, You are my King Almighty.
I worship You, my King on the throne.
I worship You, King Almighty.
I worship You, King in authority.

Contents

Acknowledgments

With special thanks to my bishop and overseer, Stuart Smith, who has been a faithful leader, wonderful pastor, spiritual father, and an adviser in my Christian journey. Bishop Smith is one whom I can trust and depend on in times of difficult decisions in my life. He is one who has the love of God in his heart and has influenced my life in such a tremendous way. I just want to say, "Thank you, Lord, for placing Bishop Smith in my life twelve years ago!" I love you, Bishop Smith. Keep up the excellent work at Gospel Light Church; we appreciate your hard work and dedication to the kingdom of God. You make all the difference in Newark!

To my friend, sister, mother, and adviser in the Gospel Evangelist, Lucille Smith, I thank God for your spirit of gratitude and inspiration in my life. Thank you for all your ways of checking up on me with precious, loving, and concerned phone calls, which were always just on time. I love and appreciate you; keep up the excellent work in Zion. My sister, we need your encouragement more than you will ever know.

In memory of the late and beloved Mother Blanch Riley, who always encouraged me to be strong in the Lord and to hold on to Jesus, who taught me about righteous living and loving others and forgiving others no matter what, because I will not enter heaven without forgiving my brothers. Thank you, Mother Riley, for teaching me how to pray and instilling in me the values of always looking my best and eating the best foods.

To Sister Maxwell, my beloved sister and prayer partner in the Lord, oh, how I thank the Lord for bringing you into my life just on time. To my family and Bryel William, I appreciate your tremendous love.

Reflection

Dates and year shown throughout this book reflect the time and date this manuscript was written.

Introduction

Little did I know, when I gave my life to the Lord Jesus in water baptism after September 11, 2001, that my life would change so drastically. I had developed a personal and intimate relationship with my Maker that is both enjoyable and fulfilling. I have experienced His divine love, blessings, miracles, and protection in my life. This love affair is one that I know I will never experience with another human being.

The hole that I had in my heart, which I thought would never be filled, was filled with God's love after I received the Holy Ghost, on Easter of 2002. I am living and experiencing true love through the power of the Holy Ghost. God has brought me under His wings through much prayer, fasting, and reading His Word. Moreover, truly, I can say that I have experienced His miraculous power through the many encounters I have had with people of all nations.

As a born-again Christian, I believe God is still using His children to bless others as long as they are available and willing to take up the challenge. I asked God to bless me to be an encouraging child of God—one who is always ready to pray or speak the Word of God to lift someone else's spirit whether they are saved or not. I promised God to make myself available, anytime and anywhere, in order to respond to His people's needs. In asking God for this blessing, I knew it would be a great responsibility, yet I accepted the challenge, anyway. The Word of God said, "I can do all things through Christ which strengtheneth me" (Philippians 4:13).

There has never been a dull moment in my life since I met Jesus. All my days are filled with assignments, and this brings about tests and deliverance. I am always seeking for the next adventure God has for me; I live for these moments as they bring joy to my soul. In my quest for a closer intimate relationship with Jesus, He has taken me above the normal realm of worshipping Him and has released me into the supernatural realm of higher heights and deeper depths.

Worshipping Jesus makes one want to stay in His presence forever. One feels so honored that he does not want to be interrupted by text messages, phone calls, or the doorbell. One wants to be able to enjoy the glory of God in His raw presence. In the presence of God, one can truly experience His power and awesomeness.

Chapter 1

The Smell of God's Presence

February 11, 2008 8:00 p.m.

Have you ever smelt the fragrance of the Almighty God? Well, let me tell you about it. God's fragrance is one I will never forget has long as I live. It is an unmistakably lovely and delightful aroma. I first encountered the essence one cold winter morning as I rested in bed. I began to talk to the Lord about it and stretched in bed, not wanting to move, afraid it would leave me. I was truly enjoying God's divine presence. However, I had to visit a dear friend, who was in the hospital. Later that afternoon, I went to visit Mother Fay, who was burnt by accident, at St. Barnabas Hospital. As soon as I entered the room, she said, "I smell the fragrance of God on you." I was amazed! The Lord had confirmed what I thought it was. Of course, I began to worship, and the anointing of God fell on me.

This anointing brought me to another level in God, and I was convinced that Jesus was preparing me for the next storm in my life. I love how the power of God makes one feel as if one can accomplish anything, and it is true, you can. I personally appreciate the scripture that says I can do all things through Christ, which strengthens me. Daily, I have used this scripture to achieve challenging tasks in my life. I have come to realize that it's not me who does the work but the Christ in me who does. I believe He has strengthened me to achieve it. According to the King James Version of the Bible, which states in the Word of God, "I can do all things through Christ which strengtheneth me" (Philippians 4:13). Once one applies the Word with faith and confidence in Jesus, the devil cannot stop you. In my fellowship with Jesus, He has led me to many people—one of whom I will tell you about. To God be the glory!

1

Chapter 2

Mrs. Ollie

February 12, 2008 6:25 p.m.

Her name is Mrs. Ollie, who was a wonderful, kind, compassionate, and God-fearing woman. My first meeting with Mrs. Ollie was at an assisted living facility where I worked. On the first day I began my job, I heard a lovely, soft voice in the hallway saying, God gives us blessings every day. I was excited; this was my kind of lady. I turned around, wanting to meet whoever this woman was speaking about my God!

I turned to see a lady with dark hair and the most fantastic smile bending over, walking with her walker. I was amazed and surprised to see that she was not an African American woman but one of Arabic descent. Immediately, I fell in love with Mrs. Ollie.

I had the pleasure of having Mrs. Ollie, as a client; and on her good days, we spent countless amounts of hours singing old hymns in the mornings and afternoons. Together we went through our daily struggles. Mrs. Ollie has been an inspiration and a tower of "strength" in my life since I first met her. Yet there were days when she was so sick, and the Lord used me to sing, pray, and comfort her. She gladly welcomed the prayers. She was so comforted to know there was another believer there to assist her. God truly knows where to place His children: exactly where they are needed. The Lord has blessed her to reveal many of my gifts and talents to me. Although I enjoyed working at the assisted senior living, I sometimes had to leave early to get to my doctor's appointment, and this Thursday was no exception even though it was Valentine's Day. To God be the glory!

Chapter 3

A Date with Jesus

February 14, 2008 10:20 p.m.

That morning began with great expectation for me. It was Valentine's Day, and I had a doctor's appointment for a bone density test. I also had a date with Jesus; it was one of my many dates I set aside just to communicate with God! I went to work all dressed up in my knee-length flower dress, with white background and pink, yellow, and green flowers. In addition, my pink shoes, red felt hat, and a good-sized pink handbag. I felt and looked marvelous. While on the job, there were lots of excitement and gift giving.

Oh, how I wish God's people could live like this every day; happy and loving one another and showing their affections. I left work at 1:30 p.m. and headed west on Route 22, to my appointment at a medical facility. I just had enough time to make my 2:30 p.m. appointment in Berkeley Heights, New Jersey. I headed up to the windy road after getting off the highway, worshiping and shouting, "Hallelujah," all the while; the anointing of God encouraged me. I reached the parking lot and parked in lot 3, just as my mother instructed me to do. Because she worked there, I was excited that God had a plan for me to be here today. I turned seven times under the influence of the Holy Ghost before I went into the building, which is a sign of deliverance.

As I made my way to the front desk and asked for directions, I greeted everyone in my path with a "God bless you." Ultimately, I had to use the restroom. As I entered the restroom, there was a Hispanic woman standing by the sink. I greeted her, and she greeted me back. I realized she was distressed over something, and I asked her if she was all right. She told me that her sister had cancer and was in the hospital. I listened to her silently. Realizing that this was the purpose I was sent here—because I can remember, after the doctor told me, I may have osteoporosis, I too felt overwhelmed and had to patiently sit in my car and ask God if all was well with me—I know I had to pray with her. We embraced each other and prayed for her sister's healing as the Lord led me. She began to cry as I prayed. We then said good-bye to each other. I was once again on my journey and asked someone for directions. The first direction I received was wrong, and then I was given another set of directions, which led me to the right office. There a friendly face greeted me. In fact, I had asked the Lord to bless me with Christ-like people. I was given some forms to fill out with lots of medical questions, most of which I have not a clue about. After I had given back the forms, immediately, a tall white woman in her forties came from a side door and called me by my name to follow her.

Susan, as it turns out to be, was her name. She took me to a large room filled with equipment after she introduced herself. She told me to put my belongings on the chair and showed me a large piece of equipment. I had to lie down after removing my hat and shoes. That was when Susan began to question me. "Marie, did you come from work?"

"Yes," I responded. Susan was still trying to get more acquainted with me.

"Marie, why are you coming from work dressed up like that?"

I said, "I have a date with the Lord."

Susan asked again, "Marie, are you going to church?"

"No," I replied, "I have a date with God, you know, like with your spouse, friend, or children." Susan was shocked!

"I do know God! But I never spend special time with him."

I turned around and asked Susan in bewilderment, "I can't believe you never had a date with God?"

She said, "Not like that."

In short, I realized God wanted to open Susan's spiritual eyes as to how every one of us shared a unique relationship with him. That night, as I rested in bed and reflected on my meeting with Susan and the Hispanic woman in the restroom, it dawned on me how much God loves His people and wants them to have a personal relationship with Him. I dozed off, wondering what excitement the Lord had planned for me next. To God be the glory.

Chapter 4

A Ride to Bible Class

February 22, 2008 1:33 p.m.

One Wednesday night, just as I was about to give up on going to Bible class, after I was already excited and told the Lord I was going. I decided I could only go if I got a ride from my sister in Christ because I was too tired to drive. However, to my delight, she too was in need of support to go to church that night. In fact, that is when I recognized that God sometimes uses me in simple ways to bless others. Here I was, thinking I needed help, and she too was in need. However, God turned it around that night and used her tremendously to bless me and blow my mind. Let me tell you what happened: when my friend showed up to drive me to church, I hurried downstairs because the phone was ringing, and I knew it was her calling, yet I did not answer. I just took it for granted that she was calling to tell me she had arrived.

Nevertheless, to my surprise, when I opened the door, I was greeted with the most beautiful sight I ever seen.

"Wow, wow," I exclaimed! Her son stood with a gorgeous big bunch of flowers and roses, smiling. The sight of him holding the flowers was the cutest picture anyone would ever want to see.

He said, "We appreciate you," with a great big smile.

Boy, was I in shock. I hugged and kissed and squeezed him. I ran back upstairs, talking to the Lord, and I said, "You did this! What are you up to next?" I was smiling the whole time. Jesus had just turned my day around and told me how much He loved and appreciated me through my friend and her son. In addition, God used us both to bless each other that night.

In church that night, there was a rejoicing at Zion. Even before my friend showed up, I promised the Lord, if I made it to church, I was going to rejoice. This leads me into another extraordinary purpose God had planned for me. I would like to tell you about a friend of mine named Mr. Bill, who is a compassionate and caring human being. To God be the glory!

Chapter 5

God's Blessing Through Mr. Bill

March 1, 2008 9:03 p.m.

He is the owner of a school, and he treats the children with such love and respect, you would believe they were his. In fact, he doesn't have any children. Mr. Bill is compassionate in many ways; daily, I watch as parents, students, and teachers go to his office for counseling. He always makes time for them even when he is leaving for a rehearsal or recital. Mr. Bill is caring and unselfish. I can remember about two years ago, when I decided to go back to college and finish my education, the Lord used him as a vessel to bless and encourage me.

I was taking piano lessons at the time and had decided to end them to save money for my college tuition. I was talking to the Lord about paying my rent and tuition fees, which was impossible for me. You see, both were due at the same time, and I was financially unable to pay for them. Then, I reminded the Lord about how, four years ago, He blessed me to miraculously only pay $8 for rent. This miracle happened on more than one occasion when I moved to Florida. All while I was not working even though every day I would go out to seek for a job. In doing this, I was depending upon the Lord to take care of my rent. In addition, I mentioned to the Lord that I would pay the piano fee. For some reason, I opened my mouth and said to the Lord, "If only Mr. Bill knew my financial situation, he would help me because I knew him to be a very generous person."

Moreover, the Lord would send me to the school early before my lessons, to pray for the students, teachers, parents, and the staff. I was certainly favored to have a key to the school. This opportunity allowed me to pray throughout the school, without interference from anyone, three times or more a week. I enjoyed these afternoons with the Lord. However, one day, as I approached the school, I noticed that the owner's car was there. I began to ask the Lord why he was there so early. I could sense God was up to something, but he did not respond. As I walked into the building slowly and hesitated, not sure what was going on, I saw Mr. Bill in the main office.

I knew something was wrong, but I waited for him to speak. He told me about the need for more students and the financial issues the school was having. In my heart, I was excited. I knew God was going to do a miracle! I told him to let us pray. We simply asked the Lord to bless us with more students for piano and voice lessons. By the following week, every day I went home, there was a message from the school that God was sending new student of all ages. I ran around my apartment for each student God sent. By the end of the week, God had given us seventeen students. I took great pleasure in running around my apartment seventeen times, plus some, and thanked the Lord for His blessings.

Another amazing thing the Lord did at the school was that He opened the school door, which was locked. It all started while I was on the job that day and felt this powerful anointing. I was babysitting and asking the Lord if I really have to go for my piano lesson that day. Although, I enjoyed piano lesson, I was tired and wanted to go home. However, the Spirit of the Lord was encouraging me to go, and I told Him, "All right."

From the parking lot, I could see the owner and the staff trying to open the school door but could not, and I began to pray. I asked the Lord to help them open the door. I had decided I was not getting out of the car until the door was open. I then began to read my favorite scripture, (Isaiah 54) I felt the Spirit of the Lord tugging at my heart to look towards the door, and they were entering. I kindly thanked the Lord; although I was not aware of the situation with the door, I knew the Lord would have opened it for me, because He told me to go to piano lesson. Later, as I entered the building, the owner was sitting in the secretary's seat, and I said, "Good afternoon, sir." He leaped from around the desk and started to thank God! His story was, they did not have the key to the door; and they were trying other ways to open it, but they could not. However, as soon as I came, the door flew open. Now, looking back on the extraordinary miracle God had done, I should not have been surprised as to what was going to happen next. What happened after that turned out to be a blessing that proves all things are possible with God when you ask and believe in faith.

As I entered the school with much faith in God, I said, "I am blessed by the owner who greeted me." Moreover, I was shocked to see him working at the front desk at this time since usually it's the secretary at that hour. I should have known that God was up to something. He really caught me off guard. Mr. Bill asked how much was my tuition balance—since there was an annual fee, and it was the end of my first year at the music school. I looked up and said, "Lord, help me!"

Mr. Bill did the most unbelievable thing and said to his assistant, "Mr. Steve, tell her the tuition balance."

I looked to God again. What was wrong with him, I thought, he is the owner, and the balance is in the computer, why am I going to a room with Mr. Steve?

Nevertheless, I went with him. The owner's assistant said, "God told Mr. Bill to tell you you're balance is zero. From now on, you don't have to pay for piano lessons!"

I asked, "What?" And he said, "Your tuition balance is zero."

I thought, Lord, what is this? The Lord spoke to me then and said to stop rushing my lessons and take my time. I laughed, laughed some more, and the more I laughed, the more the anointing fell on me, until Mr. Steve and Mr. Bill came to the room, laughing, and tried to calm me down. That evening, I did not have any piano lessons because I could not concentrate. I was amazed at what the Lord had done for me. He used Mr. Bill in such a unique and profound way to bless me. In addition, to the various miracles, God had revealed His power to me. He has taken me around the world to discover even more of His glory! Coming up in the next chapter, how my God used me to bless my friend, and in return, He used her to surprise me. To God be the glory!

Chapter 6

A Surprise from the Lord

March 2, 2008 5:55 p.m.

I would like to tell you about a blessing that the Lord surprised me with, about two years ago. It first began at a birthday dinner party for my mother and aunt at a Chinese buffet in Plainfield, New Jersey. We were enjoying a pleasant dinner, and the conversation was great. All of a sudden, I burst out, "How about a family reunion cruise?" My family was dumbfounded, "A cruise? We cannot afford it." In fact, some of them responded and said, "I am afraid of water."

They were all against the idea; imagine, young and old alike, all had no confidence in God or themselves. I had a difficult time, trying to persuade them that we can afford it and that the Lord would provide if we put our trust in Him. I told them there was nothing to be scared about, and "Let us give it a try," but they all insisted no. Instead, they wanted a local trip in the United States. By then, I had enough of their doubts and fears. That's when I said, with a lot of faith in God, "I am going, God is able, and I have faith He will provide for me. In my heart, I knew God already made the provisions for me, and I was determined to see the blessing come to pass." Nevertheless, we went on with our dinner.

The evening ended, and we all hugged each other. That night, my spirit was so stirred, and I was so excited, going home, anticipating a cruise from the Lord. I wrote to the Lord and asked him to bless me with a cruise. Later, when I got home, I also went on my knees and prayed to God, thanking him for my vacation!

About two weeks later, I was on my way out the door to jog on a Sunday morning, and the phone rang. I answered it, and there was a lovely voice on the other end of the phone, saying, "Sister Marie, do you know anyone who would like to go on a cruise?" I began to jump up and down yelling, "Me, me, and me." Right away, I knew it was God who had answered my prayer. When I calmed down, I recognized the voice to be my church sister, and she said, "Are you sure?"

I said, "Yes, yes." I ran out the house, saying, "Thank you, Lord," and I ran all the way to the park; and during my five-mile run, all I was saying was, "Thank you, Jesus!" That was the fastest five miles I ever ran in my life. I literally flew home and showered because I was going to pick up the sister to get further information about my cruise on the Princess.

In fact, I had to go to Suffern, New York, to meet the mother and daughter, who were paying for my trip. It turned out that all expenses were paid for me. In addition to going to New York, I told my pastor and family about my blessing, and they were all shocked because my dreams manifested. Right away, I loved the elderly mother, who was named Mrs. Evelyn. I noticed she had a very thankful spirit.

I came to realize the reason for this gratitude was because all their lives, they had traveled on cruises. Yet, the mother had never been through the Panama Canal, and this was her last chance to travel due to her physical disabilities. I realized, the Lord was using me to fulfill her final wish to travel. While I was down in Suffern, visiting the family, they made mention about how they still could not believe that I could go with them on the cruise in such a short notice. That's when I began to tell them about my desire to go on a cruise, and I knew this was God's answer to my prayers. In fact, that's the time, Katrina, the storm, decided to hit us. We waited for the next two days for it to go by so we could depart from Newark Airport. To our dismay, the next morning was a disaster; the airport was closed, and Katrina was still going strong.

We stayed home and watched the news with horror and dismay because the following day, we had to travel to Newark airport. Nevertheless, I knew I had to keep faith. Mrs. Evelyn and her daughter kept asking me if I believed we will still be able to go on the cruise since our flights were cancelled. I said yes because I was trusting in God, who is the author and finisher of my faith.

The next morning, Mrs. Evelyn asked me if we should still go to the airport. I said yes, and lo and behold, when we reached the airport, our flight was on the chart; but later, we watched as they eventually cancelled it. As we took the journey back home, I was still focused and said, "It was better to be safe than sorry." While at home with my new friends, "I suggested we a play a game called cruise; that's when we pretended that we were on the Princess, dining and having conversation with other people. We enjoyed this game because it helped us to pass the time and uplifted our faith in God!

The next day, sure enough, we were on our way again. Mrs. Evelyn still asked me again if I believe it's possible we will make the cruise, I said yes! I was even more encouraged because all the while, I was in close contact with God. In fact, I prayed and reminded God that He gave me this opportunity, and nothing was going to hinder me. In addition, I called my pastor during the ordeal, and he prayed for me, without me even asking him to. The prayer he prayed increased my faith in God. I was also healed from a side pain I had. Amen! Sure enough, we made it.

It was a great sight at Newark Airport when we finally arrived that morning. It seemed as if people from all walks of life were there trying to catch a plane to get out of Newark. However, we were excited and exchanged stories with other passengers about how we had to endure the storm and how many times we came to Newark Airport and had to return home. Mrs. Evelyn's daughter kept repeating to everyone that it was my faith in God why we were going on the cruise, because the storm had let her lose confidence in going. To our delight, all of us were in the same boat. Yet, some people were worse off than us, those who were staying or living in Florida, because they had no electricity.

After leaving Newark, we landed in Orlando, Florida. For the first time, I could see what the other passengers were talking about at Newark Airport: there was still no electricity available, and the taxi driver had to be very careful when he was driving. Of course, not to mention the damages that were so evident in the city. I kept praying the entire way for our safety and for the city's restoration. We got to the ship safely.

While aboard the Princess, I was astonished at the beauty of the ship. We were all excited to board and looked forward to seeing our balcony rooms that overlooked the sea. I wanted to explore right away, but my friends wanted to eat. They were so happy to show me all the wonderful foods that were available to us, and they were right; the food was delicious, and the dining arrangement was fabulous. For me, the excitement was the fresh air and the hot spa. I would get up in the mornings and jog on the deck; it was lovely. However, one day, our toilet was clogged; and when I called maintenance, they did not come. Eventually, I did the next best thing and prayed, and to my delight, the Lord unclogged the toilet. I laughed so hard, and I was beside myself to see that God was God; no matter where I was, He answered my prayers.

Furthermore, our trip took us to Jamaica, Costa Rica, and Panama. Because Katrina had damaged the port of Cozumel, Mexico, that part of our trip was cancelled. To say the least, I did not miss that part of the trip; I enjoyed myself. Until this day, I believe it was not God's will for us to have traveled there. I felt as if I was a princess aboard the ship. Each night, I was escorted to my table with my friends to dinner. It was the ship's tradition to have their male staff perform this act. The food was so delicious, and with so many favorite dishes to choose from, it was really hard for me to pick. I thought, Lord, what I did do to deserve this?

While aboard with my friends, the daughter told me, I had to stay onboard with her mother while she would take an excursion trip in Jamaica. I was surprised because she did not mention it before we left their home. I felt in my heart that it was unfair, yet I told her okay. I prayed and reminded the Lord that this was my home country, and it was one of the main reasons why I was so excited about the trip. In reality, I came to realize that God is an awesome God, and He specializes in "the things that are impossible." Later, my friend told me it was okay; she would take her trip to Costa Rica, and I could go and enjoy Jamaica. I enjoyed handing out tracts to the people on the cruise ship and in Jamaica. Not only did God use me in an extraordinary way to bless this family, but He also used them to bless me.

Meeting people from all around the globe and learning about other's cultures and religions was especially intriguing for me. One day, while having lunch in the dining area, we began to introduce ourselves to each other and shared our experiences about Katrina. This was a big topic every day at the dining table. Each person wanted to know how we coped with the storm. A lady mentioned how she lost her ring. It was at that moment that I took the opportunity to mention to the lovely group that we should all pray and ask God for a miracle. To my delight, everyone at the table held hands and prayed. I enjoyed every moment of my time while aboard the Princess—to the point where I wished I could have stayed longer. The captain's party was fabulous. That is where you were granted the privilege to meet and dine with the captain. I took the time to take a picture with the captain because I promised Sam, my spiritual child, that I would grant him this request. Formal nights were a delight to experience because we wore our finest clothes. We enjoyed the company of others and their excellent conversation. I learned more about other cultures and how they were able to afford to take this cruise.

For instance, I met a lady from Jamaica who asked me who I was traveling with. I told her my story. She was shocked and said, "I can't believe it." She then mentioned how she and her church family put their trip together and how costly it was. Surprisingly enough, that was when my eyes opened up! And it was then that I was able to see just how much my trip cost and how much my God loves me. To God be the glory!

Chapter 7

My Bone Density Test Results

March 8, 2008 8:25 p.m.

About a week ago, I wrote about going to a medical group and having a bone density test done just to make sure I did not have osteoporosis. On February 5, 2008, I had my annual checkup, and while the nurse was taking my height, she said out loud, "You are five feet three."

And I said, "No, that's not my height! I am five point five feet and a half inch."

And she was angry but remeasured me. Then she said in a rude voice, "You are five feet three," and showed me the gap on the scale, between five point five feet and a half inch and five feet three.

And I still insisted, "I have been five point five feet and a half inch all my life."

She replied in frustration and said, "Talk to the doctor when he comes." I was shocked at her behavior, as if I did not know my own height. Then I began to focus on God and asked Him, "Did you do allow this?"

The doctor came in and asked how I was doing. I said, "Blessed doctor," but the nurse just told me, I am five three, and I have always been five point five feet and a half inch.

The doctor took a look at my chart from a year and a half ago and said, "Marie, you are five point five feet and a half inch." Then he said, "Step on the scale, she might have made a mistake." He measured me frontward then backward, and lo and behold, the doctor was also shocked. "Marie, this concerns me," he said. "You are five three," and he sat me down and asked if anyone in my family has osteoporosis.

All the while the doctor was talking to me, I was saying in my heart, "The devil is a liar. I knew I was in the best health possible in my life because it was over four years now that the Lord has granted me a miracle to take off fifty-seven pounds. I was currently a part-time student and a full-time employee. I could not possible handle such a bad news. I thought to myself, was I supposed to lose my mind, and if this news were true, who would take care of me? As these thoughts ran through my mind, the voice of faith spoke to me and said this must be my assignment. I then realized I had too much faith in God for him to allow this to happen to me. I realized, there must be a purpose why I was placed in this situation, and I needed to talk to the Lord in private. After making an appointment for a bone density test, which was scheduled on Valentine's Day, I went outside, in my car, and had a talk with the Lord. I asked Him if He was allowing this and if I was okay, and the Lord answered yes to all my questions. I then said, "Lord, you must have a purpose for doing this, like blowing the doctor's mind or people along the way you want to bless." I was excited and was relieved for the confirmation. I was safe in the arms of Jesus. I only told one person, and I told her the Lord said I was fine.

March 9, 2008 9.00 p.m.

This brings me back to why I went for my bone density test. Well, I got my result in the mail a week later, and I went back to the doctor. I was puzzled as to my results being excellent. Yet, my doctor was not worried as to why I had shrunk, so there I was in the doctor's office. He confirmed that my bone density test was excellent, and as a matter of fact, I had bones of a twenty-year-old. He also mentioned, I had double bones (which was unusual) and that I was in excellent health. He mentioned that he had never seen such a thing in all his practice and was amazed. But my question was not yet answered, so I asked the doctor what about my height. That's when he said, "Get on the scale." I did, and my doctor looked shocked, and I asked, "What's my height, doctor?"

He began to say, "Well, Marie, maybe we used the wrong scale, or we were not precise on your prior visit—"

I interrupted him and said, "Well, doctor, what is my height? He began to say, "Last time you were here, you were five three," and I realized he was beating around the bush. So I insisted, "How tall am I now?" My doctor went on about when I was there a month ago my height was five three, and I asked him again what it is now. By then, I had enough of the devil's tricks.

That is when my doctor told me, I was now five feet four inches tall. I jumped off the scale and said, "God gave me my miracle. Just this morning, I asked the Lord to bless me, so I would have grown taller than when I had first visited my doctor." I said, "Doctor, from the time you told me, I shrunk, I went to God and asked Him if this was His doing, and He said yes."

The doctor could do nothing else but agree. I told him, "God is going to bless me to grow back to my original height." Through all my adventures with God, I never knew what challenges or tests would face me next, yet I met them head-on with faith in God. The lesson I learned from this is that, "God is truly no respecter of person," and if He has to use me in such a profound way, to open up my doctor's eyes for him to remember that God still does miracles, well, that's fine with me. In the next chapter, I was stranded on the road one snowy morning, but God showed up for me. To God be the Glory!

Chapter 8

Trouble Struck on My Way to Work at 5:00 AM

March 9, 2008 9:25 p.m.

One morning, last semester, I was on my way early to work because I start work at 6:00 a.m. However, I never made it to work. Boy, was I in for a shock! That morning, as I turned the corner, I heard a loud sound. I thought to myself, this could not be coming from my car! I was shocked, yet I knew it was my car because I was the only one on the road at that hour, 5:45 a.m.

I had to think fast: instantly, the car stopped dead in the middle of the road once I turned the corner. "What was I to do?" I asked myself because no one was in sight. I looked around and decided I needed to push the car out the road. Then a scripture came back to me: God is my helper. If God was my helper, what did I have to worry about but to trust Him and believe He would send help to deliver me? According to the King James Version of the Bible, in the book of Isaiah, verse 41 states, "Fear thou not; for I am with thee: be not dismay for I am thy God: I will strengthen thee; yea, I will help thee; yea I will uphold thee with the right hand of my righteousness" (Isaiah 41).

I just had it preached to me on Sunday. Therefore, I jumped out the car and looked under the hood, yet all the while, I knew it was my hassle. Right away, a car came down the road, so I stopped it and asked the driver for help. To my delight, he said yes. However, he continued to drive down the road. I said, "Lord, where is he going?" but it did not bother me because I knew that God was on my side. I looked for help across the street; a couple was coming out of their house, and I ran to ask them if I could use their phone, yet I was turned down.

"We have to catch our bus," they said. Then I asked them to call a friend and tell her what happened to me. Suddenly, to my surprise, I saw the man I asked for help coming back down the road towards me. He then told me, he went to park his car because he lived down the street. Consequently, I had to borrow his phone to call my office. The Good Samaritan, that's what I called him. He helped me push the car into a parking spot close-by. Then he took me home, but all I could think about was how was I getting to college to take my finals because I was the first one to speak that morning. As a result of that, as soon as I got in the house, my friend called and said she was just a few blocks from my house. I told her to come and get me, and she agreed to take me to work after dropping her son to school.

Throughout my stay at my friend's house, I began to talk to the Lord. I reminded Him of how faithful I had been to Him and how I always used my car to help others. As a matter of fact, just yesterday, I was using the car to deliver food for the poor and needy. I also participate in a food drive sponsored by the music school, which held a concert in Plainfield, New Jersey, at the YMCA. In fact, just as I finished asking the Lord to bless me with a car to borrow, my friend approached me from her bedroom door and said, "Sister Marie, do you want to borrow my mother's car?" Immediately, I knew the Lord heard my cry for help.

Without even knowing me, my friend's mother loaned me her car to get to school. If that was not my Daddy, Jesus, working out His perfect plan for me, then I do not know what else it could be. However, she told me, I had to return it by 2:30 p.m. I was so thankful; I had more than enough time to get to class and back. Only one small problem, I was not used to her car. I had to cry out to God for help again! As if that was not bad enough, while driving to class, the news reporter reported that there was an accident on parkway south my exit! I said to the Lord, "You did not bring me this far to leave me now." For a while, I went into some serious intercessory prayer and worshipped the Lord for the lanes to clear up. Surely, as I prayed and worshiped, I began to watch the lanes ahead clear up. God began to move on my behalf, and eventually, He cleared my way totally. By this time, I was giving God the glory by shouting and worshipping saying, "Hallelujah," all the way to school.

God had given me the victory. That morning, the Lord told me to speak on what happened to me instead of my topic about the poor and needy. I realized, he had increased my faith and that nothing was impossible with God once you believe and trust in Him. In addition, He uses my circumstance to bless my classmates: some were unbelievers and appreciated the speech. Those who where Christian were shocked by my speech and were enlightened by it! As a result of this, I finally got my A in public speaking class. Because I always got an A-, but God turned it around in my favor. In the end, I thanked God that He is always working through my life to bless others. I know the next episode will be very enlightening relating to the senior assisted living that I mentioned in previous chapters. To God be the glory!

Chapter 9

A Beautiful Lady

March 14, 2008 3:00 p.m.

During my many years of working at the assisted living for seniors, I have met some interesting people, but this particular individual and employee was the most dedicated person I have ever met. She inspired me in ways I never dreamed of; her devotion to the residents was incredible. While on her deathbed, she asked me how her residents were doing and said to me, "I want to go back to work."

This first encounter began one day when I stepped into the break room at work. There was a beautiful Spanish woman sitting at the table. She seemed tired, and I asked her what was wrong, and she told me, she had a deadly disease called lupus.

Of course, I did not fully understand what lupus was. Yet I encouraged her in the Lord, asked if she believed in God and if she had faith in God, and sure enough, she did. It was this faith in Almighty God, which would keep her until she left this world. Her name was Maria, and she explained and told me what lupus was. I remember praying for my co-worker and asking God to heal her body, not knowing it was just the beginning of my prayers for her and our friendship and changes to come at the assisted senior living.

During my friend's sickness, she was always at work even with an oxygen tank. Her duties were changed to suit her capability to work. At her worst times, she was present at her post. I can recall one summer how it was extremely hot, and she showed up to work at the front desk. I was shocked and amazed at her tenacity. I went up to her and asked if she was okay because she did not seem well to me. She just smiled and said, "I am okay."

About a month or so later, she was at the hospital again. Nonetheless, this time she was at the ICU. As soon as I heard the news, I decided I would visit. My co-workers told me that only family members could go and see her. Yet, the Lord was dealing with my heart to go visit her. It was on my mind all day; although I mentioned Maria's situation to my co-workers, they refused to come with me to see her. I had to call a friend to go with me. To my surprise, she too said, if only families are allowed, they will not let us in.

I had to remind my friend about the God we served and that my faith is in God. We went that evening to visit my co-worker, but before we went in the hospital, we prayed for the Lord to clear the way. The Lord did clear the way for us because the person at the front desk did not ask us any questions when we arrived. Upon arriving in ICU, the sight of the family and the room where Maria lay was grim and felt heavy. The family was there at her bedside, which I loved immediately. Maria was hooked up to so many tubes and machines, I could hardly recognize her. Even though I was not accustomed to them, I hugged everyone and introduced my friend.

I had never seen such a sight, but my co-worker recognized my face, and she signaled in sign language that she loves me. While we were there, she signed to all her family members and struggled to write to us her dying wishes, what she wants us to accomplish in life. After which, my friend and I prayed and prayed until God Almighty came down in that room. The atmosphere changed in the room, and my co-worker's countenance was amazing. Her family members were thankful and said they felt better.

The following day, God answered our prayer for a miracle by blessing her to be moved to a regular room. The next few days, I went to the hospital often and encouraged my co-workers to visit if they loved her. Many took the opportunity and were blessed to see our co-worker. During this time, I was fasting and praying on a daily basis, and the Lord provided a ride for me each time I visited. Sad to say, she passed away, and her last words to me were, "Thank you, thank you," when I visited on the Sunday after church. However, I did have a vision of my co-worker that Tuesday morning at 4:00 a.m., right before she died. I saw her leap up in the bed and sit up. Her family was all around her.

Later that morning, when I went to work, I was told that Maria passed away at 4:00 a.m. Nevertheless, this did not come as a surprise because as I mentioned earlier the Lord had already revealed it to me in a dream. Although, her death was a very devastating occurrence. At the end, Maria had her heart's desire by having all of her family by her bedside just as it was shown to me in the vision.

The death of my co-worker brought so many of us at the assisted senior living closer together; those who did not like or speak to each other were on speaking terms. Many co-workers who criticized me for being a Christian started to tell me, they were sorry they judged me. Consequently, the barriers were broken down. I was simply doing what the Lord had placed in my heart. Still, there is another experience I had with God that marveled me so much that I wish others could enjoy an awesome experience like it.

Chapter 10

A Special Mother

March 15, 2008 1:00 p.m.

Mother Beth was the biggest encourager in my life when I first entered the church as a sinner. My first encounter with her was phenomenal. However, I am sorry to say, she has passed away. Upon my arrival to the church, I noticed an elderly mother with an amazing smile. Yet it was not her smile that brought my attention to her but the way her hands were always up in the air worshiping God. I immediately wanted what she had although I did not know what it was. I did not see anyone else in the congregation like her; she was one of a kind. I asked myself how she could be that old and keep on worshipping with her hands in the air like that.

Well, I was soon to find out: the driving force behind mother Beth's praise! Mother Beth loved God with such a passion that I wanted to be like her. However, I got to know her better one Sunday, when she shared her songbook with me; from that day on, we developed a close relationship. As a result, we exchanged telephone numbers; and my first conversation with her over the phone, I was in shock. I listened while this woman of God told me about myself and the situation I was going through without me ever mentioning a word to her. As a matter of fact, I never got to say anything during our first few conversations on the phone. I just listened and was amazed. She was revealing my life, without me telling her. How did she know what I had been through and still going through? The question I asked myself was, "Who told her?" Many years later, after I was matured in Christ and was seeking Him, God later revealed to me she, was a prophetess, similar to Anna mentioned in the Bible.

Mother Beth became my prayer partner; every time I called her, or she called me, we would pray. I believe that is how I grew in prayer and loved to pray. She always gave me godly advice and stated, God truly loves me and that I should hold on to Him. Mother Beth also told me to eat the best foods available and always look my best at all times. I took these instructions to heart, knowing they came from God. I went through a transitional period in God where Mother Beth was warning me of the devil coming in my life. I was a babe in Christ and full of zeal for God.

Yet, I could not comprehend the warnings, so I got in trouble. Mother Beth, being eighty-four years old, got down on her knees in her living room and cried out to God for my deliverance. She later told me after I returned to New Jersey, how she kept on praying for me to return. I cried out to God and thanked Him for the love He had given her for me, and never had I met someone who was so fond of me. I still speak to the Lord daily about her. The memories of her words always come back to comfort me. Many things she told me then I did not understand; however, now God has given me understanding in what she was advising and warning me of: the things that would occur in my future. She emphasized how impossible it was to serve God without faith. She also told me how to pray and ask God to let me see myself as He sees me. As well as, she saw Christ in me. I went home and cried that day because I could not possibly see how she could see Christ in me; I was so unworthy. That was the most beautiful thing anyone had ever said to me. Sure enough, I asked the Lord to reveal how He sees me. As a result of that, I am able to see myself daily the way my heavenly Father sees me, and this revelation has made me content.

However, I am happy to say that the Lord also used me to bless her in her final days on earth. I spent a lot of time with her in the hospital, praying, reading the Bible, and singing to her. I can recall during her final days at the nursing home and not having all her children accounted for, she told me to pray and ask God to send them now. I realized, she knew she was dying. I too wanted them to be by her bedside. I had such love and compassion for her that I told the Lord, as if He did not know that it was an urgent call for her. God did send all of them for her. During the time of her passing, I was home that morning, sleeping, and the Lord woke me up for my usual morning prayer at 4:00 a.m. As I got out of bed, there was this heavy burden on one of my foot. I could barely walk; I lay on the floor and began to pray for her. I began to sing and groan; I knew something was happening in the spiritual realm. Later, when I heard the news of her passing, I called her daughter right away to comfort her. I asked her what time her mom died, and she told me, 4:00 a.m. I told her what was happening to me during that time while I was praying. She told me that I was feeling the burden of her mom leaving.

To God be the glory!

Chapter 11

Miracles

March 17, 2008 7:00 p.m.

Today I am especially happy! I just got good news from one of my friends that she is going to be a grandmother. At last, after a few miscarriages, her daughter is expecting again. The Lord has blessed her daughter to be pregnant again after being led by the Lord for over a year into her office to testify of His goodness toward me and others I had prayed for.

I first came to this revelation by a conversation we had, where I was asked by her to pray for the Lord to bless her daughter to be pregnant again. You see, my friend had confidence in me that when I pray, God hears and delivers. And sure enough, God did. I prayed, "Lord, please bless my friend to be a grandmother," and I believed and waited on God.

Another good thing that made my day today was that the Lord is anointing my friend I met this semester in college. After meeting her in one of my classes for the first time, I knew she was the reason why God had placed me in this class. In fact, the Lord laid it on my heart to pray for her to receive the Holy Ghost. I had developed a relationship with her, and she told me she was Catholic. I realized she was seeking God and was influenced by the manifestation of the spirit of God when we prayed. I too was surprised at her zeal to know more about the Holy Spirit. I went home and prayed to the Lord about her zeal to know Him more. I asked the Lord to reveal Himself to her. However, it was also my prayer for her to be filled with the Holy Ghost. She was so excited, and I was grateful to God for fulfilling my heart's desire and His will for her life. What was fascinating about this miracle was that she has never been baptized before; although my friend received the gift of the Holy Spirit, she refused to be baptized at the time. However, God never gave up on her, and I kept praying for her. I realized that although I had given her scriptures to read and invited her to church, she did not fully understand what the Lord had done in her life. She also wanted to continue going to her Catholic church, and I just told her I would be praying for her. We kept in contact but lost touch after the end of the semester. However, a few years later, we reconnected; after that, I was in my apartment, interceding in prayer on her behalf. She called me and explained what was happening in her life, and I encouraged her in the Lord. She was baptized the same day we met in the name of Jesus. It is truly amazing how God works in such a mysterious way. Moreover, she had a zeal for God, and the Word of God said in Matthew 5, according to the King James Version, "Those that hunger and thirst after righteousness shall be filled" (Matthew 5:6). Shortly after that, the Lord used me to fulfill another one of His supernatural blessings at a senior assisted living. To God be the glory!

Chapter 12

One of My Favorite Residents

March 19, 2008 4:52 p.m.

Mrs. Jean is one of my favorite residents at the senior assisted living. She is very determined, outgoing, funny, wise, and faithful to God. Mrs. Jean is one of a kind. We enjoyed our morning challenges with each other, remembering and practicing words. Mrs. Jean has Alzheimer's disease. However, one morning, I had enough of my repeating the same terms to my friend and decided to ask God to intervene. That morning, I asked Mrs. Jean for my name, and she could not remember, so I started to talk to the Lord on Mrs. Jean's behalf. As I was talking to the Lord aloud, Mrs. Jean then said to me, "Are you talking to me?" And I said, "No, God." Mrs. Jean did a remarkable thing: she said in a polite manner, "I am sorry," and hung her head in reverence to God. That's how I knew she loved and feared God.

I was astonished as to how much the fear of God was in her. I asked the Lord to help Mrs. Jean with her memory because I was tired of Mrs. Jean forgetting my name every day. I realized that according to medical science, this would not be possible for my friend to continually remember my name permanently. Yet, I knew that I serve a God that is sufficient, and all things are possible with Him if I only believed in Him. After I finished praying to the Lord, I turned to Mrs. Jean and began to assist her with our daily routines. As we were leaving her room for breakfast, Mrs. Jean said my name, Marie.

I began to thank the Lord for this awesome miracle He had performed through Mrs. Jean. Not only was she able to tell me my name, but she told me everything I told her about myself. Eventually, all of her children came and visited her one day, and they were flabbergasted at her ability to remember them and past events. To say the least, one of her daughter was a host of a Christian radio talk show, and she was amazed at the miraculous work God had done through her mom. This particular daughter was a blessing because she lived faraway, and this was her first time coming to see her mother in many years. God had answered my prayer and delivered my friend. Up to this very day, Mrs. Jean knows my full name. I am just astonished at God and at how He works in us. Besides blessing Mrs. Jean with a permanent memory, God continues to show up on the job in a mighty way. To God be the glory.

Chapter 13

A Delightful Day

March 23, 2008 9:30 p.m.

Yesterday, Mrs. Ollie and myself had a delightful day, thanks be to God. My date began with me telling Mrs. Ollie it was the third day of spring; she was happy that spring had begun already. I reminded her how spring brings in new beginnings, such as, sunshine, fresh air, birds singing, and she would be going outside soon to enjoy the sun, with her short-sleeve dress. Mrs. Ollie had a glimmer in her eyes, I told her, as she often told me, "You are so cute," and kissed her all over. I wanted to just pick her up and hold her in my arms as you do with a baby. I love Mrs. Ollie so much; she is full of life and encouragement each time I see her. I mentioned to her I am seeking a new place to live, and she said, that's good.

The revelation that Mrs. Ollie gave me was that you will move. Once again, I recognized my heavenly Father speaking to me through Mrs. Ollie. I began asking Mrs. Ollie what else she would like to experience on earth since she was in her nineties, hoping to pray and ask God to grant her heart's desires before she dies. Yet all she wanted was to be comforted. I spent many days fasting and interceding for her, asking God to bless her to leave the earth without feeling pain although I did not always have her as my client. I would always leave my shift to visit her. She had been sick for a month and a half and had not been eating, but God had been keeping her by His grace and miraculous power. Everyone was amazed at her survival: nurses, staff, and family members.

However, I was not surprised because God specializes in the things that are impossible. Her time was not yet. If it were so, I would have missed my blessing yesterday morning. Upon returning to work, I was told by the staff members the next day that she almost died. Once again, God heard my prayer on my day off and kept Mrs. Ollie alive until I was able to say good-bye. Her death brought me to another level of faith in God, and God gave me the strength to encourage her family and my co-workers; as well as, I sang her favorite song at her funeral. The next incident proves to be an experience I still marvel at even today as God continues to use me to bless His people. To God be the glory!

Chapter 14

My Journey with Christ
This Summer!

April 25, 2008 10:00 p.m.

It's been a pleasure walking with God this summer on this Christian journey. After a few months of seeking the Lord for guidance, He brought me to another dimension in Him. In short, the Holy Ghost introduced me to an unusually young man this summer. One bright and sunny morning, as I opened my door (I had to rush to class), I was greeted by a young man, who said to me, "You are apostolic, aren't you?"

I was amazed. The last thing I expected was for a man to greet me in such a manner. Nevertheless, I said yes; he seemed sincere enough. In my heart, I was saying to the Lord, "Who is this?" Then he said, "I am Mr. Brown, I just move in next door with my family."

Mr. Brown turned out to be a child of God, whom God has positioned in my path to pray with and encourage. As a matter of fact, I, myself, have learned a lot from him concerning the Word of God. What was significant about this young man was that God had a ministry for him, and he is going through many tests and trials. Ever since I met Mr. Brown, he needed constant encouragement. I recognized, God sent him to call me or placed him in my path during my times of fasting and praying. For example, one evening, as I pulled up to my house and parked the car, he was there waiting. I had to pray for his deliverance because he was going through a process with immigration to get his green card.

In fact, at times, the Lord did lead me to his door to deliver a message, and when I showed up, he said, "I was praying and asking God to send me a message, and I was expecting you." We usually prayed outside, on the street, or in the hallway. Finally, after many, many months of praying and fasting, the Lord did grant Mr. Brown his heart's desire, and he received his green card. I never knew the plans God has for me, but I appreciated the people He places in my life. In fact, the next story coming up is no exception. To God be the glory!

Chapter 15

Mrs. Ann

November 15, 2010 7:00 p.m.

Yesterday, on my way home from school, I asked the Lord if I should stop at ShopRite. Yet deep down inside, I was considering the crowd because it was four days away from Thanksgiving. God said yes! I know that my time was limited because I had to be at our church day care to work. I said, "Lord, if you have a parking spot for me, I can shop."

As I entered the parking lot, I was not surprised at the traffic. Yet I persevered and searched for a spot to park near and far. After seeking for a while, I felt like leaving because there was no close parking spot available.

By now, it did not matter to me where I parked. I just wanted to park! Nevertheless, I said, "Lord, where is my parking?" Then I spotted one on the other side. By the time I got there—even though I was praying, "Lord, hold that space for me"—it was taken. I said aloud to the Lord, "I am leaving if by the time I reach the end of the parking lot, there is no empty space." I was determined I would not continue to circle the lot.

However, I found one. I went in and bought some chicken to cook for the less fortunate people at Newark Penn Station. While I was in the supermarket, the Lord started to turn me, and I said, "What is it, Lord?" He kept on turning me. I said, "I know you are doing something." Of course, from this special anointing, I expected someone to be in need of help or encouragement at any minute.

I began to pray, and then I went to pay for my groceries. On my way back to the car, I noticed an elderly white woman, who was leaning against her car, and she seems to be preoccupied. I said to the Lord, "She seems as if she is waiting for someone," and I went over to ask her if she needed any help. When I got over to her, I asked if she was alright. She said, "I am waiting for the security guard to help direct me out the parking spot." She said she had tried for about half an hour to move her car but could not get it out.

When I took a closer look, her car was extremely close to the other car. She introduced herself to me as Mrs. Ann. I told her, my name was Marie. I then asked Mrs. Ann if she had called the guard, and she said, "No, he just usually drives by." I put my hands on my hip and said, "Mrs. Ann, if that's the case, you don't have to wait on the guards to help you. I will assist you. I had such love and compassion for Mrs. Ann; she is such a dear, loving, trusting lady. I then showed her the men who usually park the cars and said, "I will call one of them to move your car." However, I remembered seeing a man on my way out of the supermarket moving the shopping carts, and he kept staring at me, and I said, "Lord, why is he staring so much?" I know I am beautiful, but I am married to you. I realized it was something more, but I did not inquire. I was trying to get to the preschool by 4:30 p.m.

Eventually, it was the same man, who was staring at me, I had to call to move Mrs. Ann's car. She was so happy and grateful when help arrived. In fact, I did mention to Mrs. Ann that I usually worked with the elderly. This was to make her feel more at ease. I gave Mrs. Ann my phone number to call me if she needs help, and she gave me her phone number. I also could not help giving her a big hug and a kiss. That's when Mrs. Ann turned to me and said to come home with her for tea. I told her, "Tomorrow because I had to be at the preschool to work."

However, Mrs. Ann insisted I follow her home to see where she lived. How great is my God, it turned out that Mrs. Ann lived in the exact direction I was heading. Another thing I realized about Mrs. Ann is that she is so trusting; while we were in the parking lot, exchanging phone numbers, she pulled out an envelope with money and told me that she just came from the bank. I advised her to put her money away carefully in her handbag. After praying to the Lord and asking Him if it was His will for me to go home with Mrs. Ann, I did follow her home. As she parked her car and began to walk toward the house with her groceries, I pulled up. However, in my heart, I knew I was supposed to help Mrs. Ann carry the bags in the house. I sat and pondered it in my heart, what the neighbor would say if they saw a strange black woman going into Mrs. Ann's house. Shortly after, I saw Mrs. Ann's fruits fell from her bags, and she did not even realize it.

Immediately, I turned my car around and parked it. I then ran to help Mrs. Ann pick up her fruits. She said to me, "I did not notice my fruits dropped." Then the real reason came to light, why I had followed Mrs. Ann home. As we approached the front door, she could not find her keys, and I ran to look in her car for them, then I checked the food bags. I had to say to Mrs. Ann, "We know for sure that you drove the car home and used the keys," and we began to laugh. Then I began to pray, "Lord, help!" That's when the Lord said, the keys were in Mrs. Ann's coat pocket, so I put my hand in her pocket and pulled out the keys. We opened the door and put Mrs. Ann's groceries in the house, and I went on my way!

I was not at all surprised when a month later—I was on my way home from Union County College—the Lord told me, I had to visit Mrs. Ann after spending seven and a half hours doing homework on the computer, and I was fasting, hungry, and tired. I had to ask Him again to make sure I was hearing right. So, I stopped by Mrs. Ann's home at 5:00 p.m. She was delighted to see me. We had tea, and while I was there, the electricity went off on the entire block, and we had to use candles. The Lord insisted I stayed with Mrs. Ann even though her daughter and granddaughter was home. In the end, I got a tremendous blessing; Mrs. Ann taught me how to knit. However, God showed up in the next chapter with His glory, and I was just amazed at the occurrence. To God be the glory!

Chapter 16

I Thank God for Preserving Me to See His Glory

November 2008

I can still remember on November 27, 2008, at 12:20 a.m., I had the pleasure of enjoying an unexpected blessing from the Lord. It was a surprise to me when I went downtown Newark to feed my children (the less fortunate men and women who live at Penn Station). Although I have been going downtown Newark Penn Station for the past thirteen years to feed the poor and needy, this is the busiest I have ever seen the traffic. I had a hard time getting through the traffic because there was a ball game taking place at the new stadium. I was frustrated as I tried to make it downtown. I had to press my way with prayer and worship; there were so many policemen directing the traffic. However, as I approached Market Street to my destination, a police directing the traffic told me to go to the other lane. I told him I needed to turn; of course, he was not pleased. On the other hand, I know I was too close to my journey to turn back, so I persevered.

Even as I pulled up my cart along the streets of Newark, police officers were all over the station. I thought to myself how the city of Newark really put out a lot of officers for one ball game. Nevertheless, I made it to my designated spot, and two police officers were standing there. I have used the same spot for thirteen years now. It was then that I decided in my heart, I am going to feed my children and will not be intimidated by anyone. While I was handing out the meals, one of the officers came and said, "That's a nice thing you are doing, and where are you from?" I told him of my church and that I have been coming downtown Newark for thirteen years now. At that moment, another police came over and joined us, and I took the time to minister to them about God's goodness. I also encouraged them to give their lives to the Lord and that I will be praying for them. Being even more inspired by the opportunity to mention God's blessings, I continued to feed my children outside Penn Station. It was then that I noticed one of the homeless men sitting on the bench inside the station, who had a beautiful bag beside him. I thought he already had his food. Yet he came and got on the line to get something to eat.

After a while, the man with the lovely bag was standing in front of me, handing the bag to me.

"Here," he said, "this is for you." So, I took the bag and looked inside it and then at his smiling face in amazement, and I said, "I cannot take it." And he said, "But you must."

He continued to insist and said, "I was at one of the churches today, and these are the foods they gave me, and I cannot cook it because I have no stove." I hesitated again, and to convince me, he said, "Well, share it with someone."

I thanked him and thought, What an amazing God I serve. At that moment, I did not know what I was going to do with the bag. However, when I looked inside the bag, there were three cans of vegetables, two-pound bag of rice, box of eggs, yogurt, frozen hot dogs, macaroni and cheese, plus other items. One thing for sure, I knew I had some cooking to do, and I must return downtown to feed my children.

In addition, I went back to speak with the officers and told them that I have been praying for them every day as my pastor had advised us to do. They were thankful for the prayers we had prayed for them. Finally, as I said goodbye to the officers and my children, l saw a man, who was in a wheelchair. I went over and handed him the last meal. As I left, he said, "God bless you." I was well on my way with my burden lightened, and he called out to me. I said in a small voice, "What is it, Lord?" He must need some money, and I had none because I never bring my handbag with me downtown. I turned and went back toward him, and as I approached him, he pulled out two one-dollar coins, and handed one to me and said, "Here is your pay." I was shocked, and smiled, and I said aloud to the Lord, "My labor has not been in vain."

Here it was, a homeless man paid me money for feeding him. I asked God if I should take it, and He said yes. So, I gladly took the one dollar. I asked God again if I could put it in the offering plate because I was on my way to Bible class. I thought, since this man was unable to make it to church to throw his offering, maybe God was using me to bring it for him! I was stunned at God's blessing for me and this man. I also thank God that He had preserved me to see His glory!

To be continued!

Thank God I've been blessed to impact the lives of the less fortunate in my community!

05.22.2012

08.25.2009

02.01.2011

01.20.2011